My First Book about the Alphabet of Dinosaurs

Amazing Animal Books Children's Picture Books

By Molly Davidson

Mendon Cottage Books

JD-Biz Publishing

Read More Amazing Animal Books

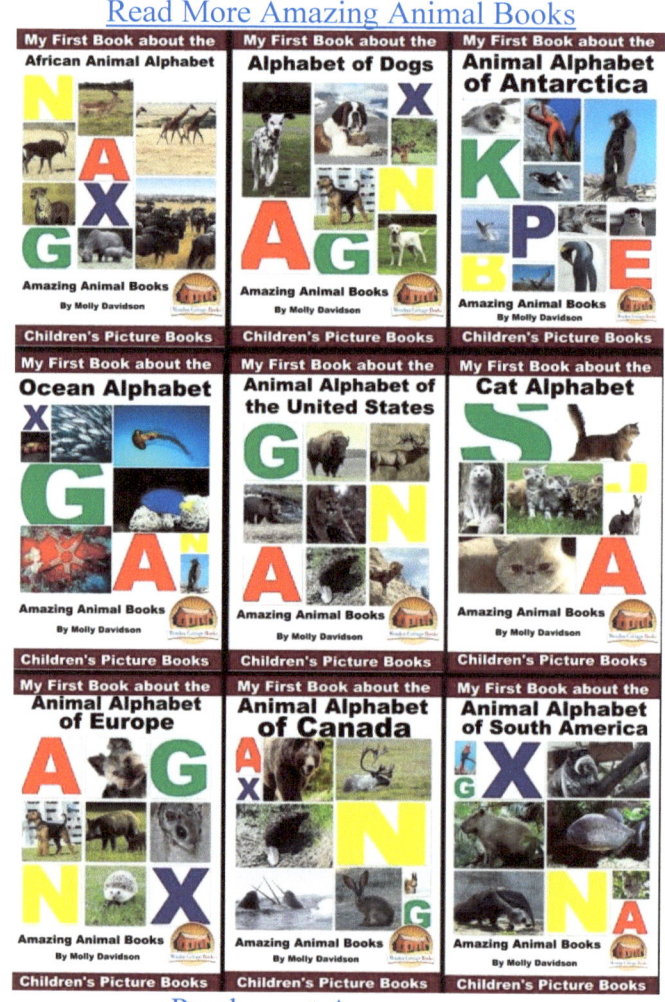

Purchase at Amazon.com

Download Free Books!
http://MendonCottageBooks.com

Introduction

The word dinosaur comes from the Greek word meaning terrible lizard.

They lived on the Earth from around 250 million to 65 million years ago, before they all became extinct.

A is for an Ankylosaurus.

Fossils of the ankylosaurus have been found in Montana and Alberta, Canada.

They had tough bony skin and a club tail that they swung to injure their predators.

A is also for an Allosaurus.

Sixty complete skeletons have been found of the allosaurus from adults to babies in Utah.

They were quick runners and meat eaters.

 is for a Brachiosaurus.

Brachiosaurus is one of the largest dinosaurs standing 50 feet tall and 100 feet long!

They used their claws for raking leaves and plants, which is what they ate.

Its front legs were longer than its back legs.

C is for a Corythosaurus.

Corythosauruses have a hollow crest on the top of their heads.

They do not have teeth in their beaks, but they do have teeth lining their cheeks, which made it easy for them to eat leaves and plants.

D is for a Dilophosaurus.

Dilophosaurus have two weak crests on their heads, which scientists think were different for girls and boys.

D is also for a Diplodocus.

Diplodocus fossils are found in the western United States.

They are some of the longest dinosaurs ever found, measuring up to 89 feet long.

They have 15 bones in their neck, and anywhere between 70 - 90 bones in their tail.

 is for an Euoplocephalus.

Euoplocephalus are the widest dinosaurs, their spikes alone measure about 6 inches each.

They grew to be about 20 feet long, with a large club on the end of their tail.

Fossils have been found in Alberta, Canada.

 **is for a Gallimimus.**

Gallimimus name means chicken mimic (copy)
and they are the fastest known dinosaur.

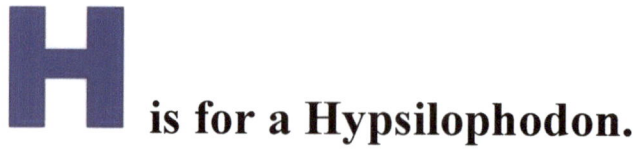 **is for a Hypsilophodon.**

Hypsilophodon fossils have been found in the United States, Spain, Portugal, and England.

They had a beak, but in the back of their mouth they also had teeth.

I is for an Iguanodon.

Iguanodons were one of the first dinosaurs to be discovered and named.

They are named iguanodon because their teeth look like iguana lizards from today.

They have a spiked thumb which scientists think they used as a weapon.

K is for a Kentrosaurus.

Kentrosaurus fossils have been found in Tanzania, Africa.

They have two rows of plates that go from their head then change to spikes halfway down their back.

L is for a Lesothosaurus.

Mariana Ruiz © <u>Wikimedia Commons</u>

Lesothosaurus are a small dinosaur, standing about 1 1/2 ft tall and weighing about 8 lbs.

They were most likely a very quick runner, since they were so small and had hollow bones, which is also how they protected themselves since they had no armor.

M is for a Malawisaurus.

Alexander Leisser © <u>Wikimedia Commons</u>

Malawisaurus is named after the place it was found Malawi, Africa.

They were 30 feet long and stood 14 feet tall.

 **is for a Nanotyrannus.**

Only one skull has been found for the nanotyrannus, meaning dwarf tyrant, and scientists are trying to figure out if it is another species of a smaller tyrannosaurus or just a baby tyrannosaurus.

O **is for an Oviraptor.**

Oviraptor fossils have been found in Mongolia, usually on top of a nest of eggs.

They have been given the nickname of the "egg thief."

P

is for a Pachycephalosaurus.

Pachycephalosaurus is a rare dinosaur that has only been discovered in Montana.

They have a 10 inch wide dome on the top of their head with 5 inch spikes surrounding it.

R is for a Riojasaurus.

Debivort © Wikimedia Commons

Riojasaurus was discovered in La Rioja, Argentina.

It has some of the largest back legs ever found.

They grew to be about 36 feet long and 16 feet tall.

S

 is for a Stegosaurus.

Stegosaurus had two rows of plates running down their back, they used these to soak up the sun when they were stood up, or to cool down when they were laid down.

They had four large spikes on their tail that they used for defense.

S is also for a Spinosaurus.

Spinosaurus stood 40 feet tall and had 6 foot spikes held up by skin on their backs.

The vertebrate, or bones in the dinosaurs back, are 20% bigger than tyrannosauruses!

T is for a Tyrannosaurus.

Tyrannosaurus was one of the largest flesh eating land animals, ever to live on the Earth.

They had powerful jaws with 7 inch tall teeth!

T is also for a Triceratops.

Triceratops was a very common dinosaur, also called the three-horned face.

The frill behind their head could grow to be over 7 feet wide.

 **U** **is for an Utahraptor.**

Zach Tirrell © <u>Wikimedia Commons</u>

Utahraptors are named after the state where their fossils have been found, Utah.

They were some of the smartest dinosaurs, and would use the claws on their hind feet to kill much larger dinosaurs.

V

is for a Velociraptor.

Velociraptor fossils have been found in groups throughout Asia.

They have a retractable claw on their back feet, which could have caused major pain to other dinosaurs.

 **is for a Wuerhosaurus.**

Pavel Riha © <u>Wikimedia Commons</u>

Wuerhosaurus were the first stegosaurus fossils to be found in China.

They stood about 9 feet tall and were 23 feet long.

Y is for a Yangchuanosaurus.

Yangchuanosaurus fossils have been found in China, measuring 33 feet in length.

They are related to Megalosaurus, the first discovered dinosaur, and Metriacanthosaurus.

 is for a **Zephyrosaurus.**

Rodney © <u>Wikimedia Commons</u>

Zephyrosaurus are a small dinosaur, standing only 3 feet tall, found in Montana.

They had rough teeth that they used for chewing plants.

Conclusion

I hope you have enjoyed reading about the amazing animals that the dinosaurs were.

One more fact, the first dinosaur was discovered in southern England in 1824.

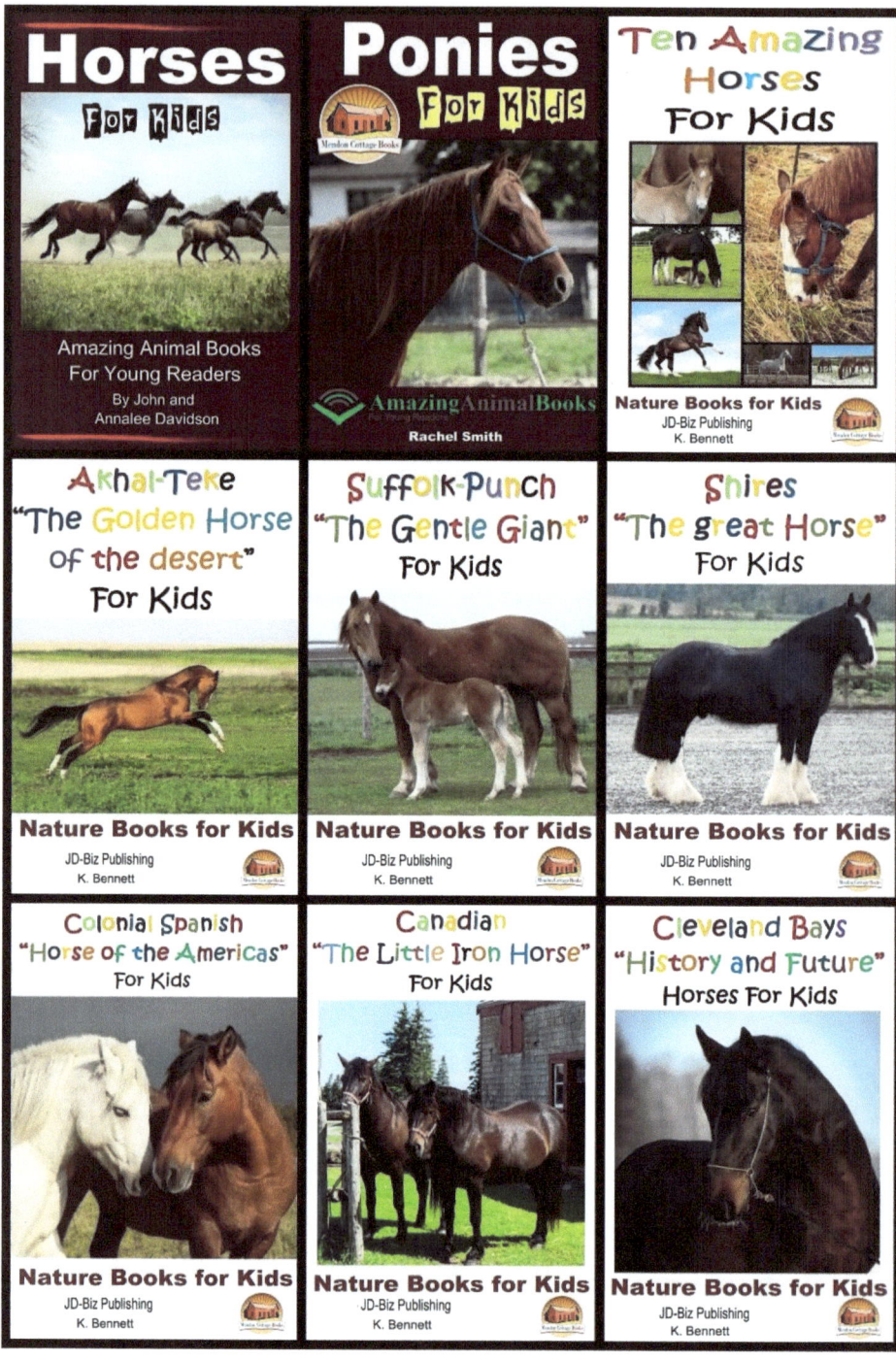

Our books are available at

1. Amazon.com

2. Barnes and Noble

3. Itunes

4. Kobo

5. Smashwords

6. Google Play Books

Download Free Books!
http://MendonCottageBooks.com

Publisher

JD-Biz Corp

P O Box 374

Mendon, Utah 84325

http://www.jd-biz.com/

www.ingramcontent.com/pod-product-compliance
Lightning Source LLC
Chambersburg PA
CBHW050902290526
45792CB00002B/670